MEDITERRANEAN DIET COOKBOOK

FOR KIDS

Young chef's Creative Cooking with Mediterranean Ingredients

Clare D. Cole

TABLE OF CONTENTS

Introduction

Greetings from the dynamic world of the Mediterranean diet, a culinary tradition known for its delicious tastes and health-promoting properties. This cookbook takes readers on a pleasant gastronomic tour of the Mediterranean region, designed especially for young, aspiring cooks. Our mission is to ignite a passion for healthy, tasty, and fresh cooking in everyone via interesting recipes, entertaining food facts, and hands-on activities.

As they set off on this culinary journey, youngsters will come across a wide variety of dishes that showcase the colorful fabric of Mediterranean civilizations. There is a gastronomic treat for every palette, ranging from traditional Italian pasta meals to flavorful Greek salads, savory Spanish tapas, and delicious Turkish desserts.

Every recipe has age-appropriate ingredients, simple-to-follow directions, and vibrant photos that are sure to spark young cooks' imaginations. We also explore the cultural influences that have molded the distinctive tastes and customs of Mediterranean food as we dig into its history and origins. Prepare yourself for a gastronomic journey that will satisfy your hunger and expand your understanding of food. Let's explore the delectable world of children's Mediterranean diet cookbooks!

Chapter 1: Breakfast

The most important meal of the day is breakfast, and kids must begin their days with a wholesome meal. Making sure your children are receiving the nutrients they need for healthy growth and development is made easier with a Mediterranean diet.

Light and refreshing, Mediterranean breakfasts often include nutritious grains, fruits, vegetables, and lean protein. These nutrients work together to provide youngsters with steady energy throughout the morning and to keep them attentive and focused.

1.1 Nuts and Berries with Oatmeal

Known for its heart-healthy properties, oatmeal is a traditional morning staple. This recipe creates a satisfying and enjoyable breakfast dish by blending the creamy sweetness of oats with the crunch of almonds and the antioxidant-rich qualities of berries.

Ingredients

- One cup of rolled oats
- Two glasses of water or plant-based or dairy milk
- ½ cup of mixed berries, including raspberries, strawberries, and blueberries
- ½ cup mixed nuts, including pecans, walnuts, and almonds
- One tablespoon of maple syrup or honey (optional)
- A dash of salt
- Half a teaspoon of cinnamon, if desired

Preparation:

1. Heat the milk or water in a medium pot until it boils.

2. After adding the oats and a little teaspoon of salt, turn down the heat to medium and simmer, stirring from time to time, for approximately five minutes.
3. Take the oats off the stove as soon as they are creamy and fully cooked.
4. If using, stir in the cinnamon.
5. Sprinkle mixed berries and almonds on top.
6. If preferred, drizzle with maple syrup or honey for extra sweetness.

Nutritional value

- ☐ Around 350 calories per serving.
- ☐ 10 grams of protein
- ☐ Fifty grams of carbs
- ☐ 12 grams of fat

☐ 8 grams of fiber

Duration of Preparation:
Ten minutes

1.2 Avocado and Eggs on Whole-Wheat Toast

Eggs are a strong source of protein, whole-wheat bread adds healthy fats, and avocado adds fiber.

Ingredients:

- A pair of whole-wheat slices

- One mature avocado
- two eggs
- One tablespoon of butter or olive oil
- To taste, add salt and pepper.
- Flakes of red pepper (optional)
- Juice from lemons (optional)

Preparation:

1. Melt the slices of whole-wheat bread until they are golden brown.
2. Melt butter or olive oil in a small skillet over medium heat while the bread is toasting.
3. Once the eggs are cracked into the pan, fry them to your desired consistency (scrambled, over-easy, or sunny side up).
4. Remove the pit from the avocado, cut it in half, and

scoop out the flesh into a dish. Using a fork, mash the ingredients and add salt, pepper, and, if preferred, a squeeze of lemon juice.

5. Over the toast, equally, distribute the mashed avocado.
6. Place a cooked egg on top of each slice.
7. If preferred, add a dash of red pepper flakes for more heat.

Nutritional value:

☐ Each dish has around 450 calories.
☐ 18 grams of protein
☐ forty grams of carbs
☐ 26 grams of fat
☐ Ten grams of fiber

Duration of Preparation:
fifteen minutes

1.3 Fruit and Granola Yogurt

This breakfast choice is a fantastic combination of creamy yogurt, sweet fruits, and crunchy granola. It is refreshing and adaptable. It's perfect as a fast snack or for hectic mornings.

Ingredients:

- One cup of plain or flavored Greek yogurt
- Half a cup of assorted fresh fruit, including apple pieces, banana slices, or berries
- One-fourth cup granola
- One spoonful of honey, if desired

Preparation:

1. Greek yogurt should be spooned into a bowl.
2. Add a variety of fresh fruit on top.
3. Over the fruit, sprinkle the granola.
4. If you would like more sweetness, drizzle with honey.

Value Nutritionally:

- ☐ Around 300 calories per serving.
- ☐ 15 grams of protein
- ☐ Grams of carbohydrates: 45
- ☐ 8 grams of fat
- ☐ Five grams of fiber

Duration of Preparation:

Five minutes

1.4 Eggs in a Scramble with Feta and Spinach

Breakfast staple scrambled eggs taste even better when topped with spinach and feta, which also improves the dish's nutritional value. This meal is a fantastic way to start the day since it's high in protein, vitamins, and minerals.

Ingredients:

- three eggs
- half a cup of freshly chopped spinach
- 1/4 cup of crumbled feta cheese and 1 tablespoon of butter or olive oil
- To taste, add salt and pepper.

Preparation:

1. Mix the eggs well with a little amount of salt and pepper in a medium-sized bowl.
2. In a nonstick skillet, preheat the butter or olive oil over medium heat.

3. Add the chopped spinach and cook for approximately two minutes, or until it wilts.
4. Transfer the eggs to the skillet and cook over low heat, turning often, until the eggs start to set.
5. After the eggs are covered with feta cheese and cooked through, they should still be tender.
6. Serve right away.

Value Nutritionally:

☐ Around 250 calories per serving.
☐ 18 grams of protein
☐ Two grams of carbs
☐ 20 grams of fat
☐ One gram of fiber

Duration of Preparation:

Ten minutes

1.5 Smoothies with Fruit

A tasty, simple, and fast way to fit a lot of nutrients into one meal is with a smoothie. You may alter this recipe by adding your preferred fruits, yogurt, or even leafy greens for an extra nutritional boost.

Ingredients:

- One cup of mixed fruit, either fresh or frozen (bananas, berries, mango)
- half a cup of Greek yogurt
- Half a cup of milk (vegan or dairy)
- One tablespoon of maple syrup or honey (optional)
- If using fresh fruit, use half a cup of ice cubes.
- One spoonful of optional flaxseeds or chia seeds

Preparation:

1. Put everything into a blender.
2. Blend till creamy and smooth.
3. Pour into a glass and start sipping right away.

Value Nutritionally:

- ☐ Around 250 calories per serving.
- ☐ 10 grams of protein
- ☐ Grams of carbohydrates: 45
- ☐ Four grams of fat
- ☐ Six grams of fiber

Duration of Preparation:

Five minutes

1.6 Whole-Wheat Pancakes with Fruit and Flour

A popular morning delight made healthy with these pancakes.

Encased in whole-wheat flour and garnished with fresh fruit, they provide a substantial amount of vitamins and fiber.

Ingredients:

- One cup of whole-wheat flour
- One-third tsp baking powder
- Half a teaspoon of salt
- One cup of milk (vegan or dairy)
- One big egg
- Two teaspoons of oil or melted butter
- One tablespoon of maple syrup or honey (optional)
- One teaspoon of optional vanilla extract
- Fresh fruit (apple pieces, banana slices, or berries) for topping

Preparation:

1. Combine the whole-wheat flour, baking powder, and salt in a large basin.
2. Mix the milk, egg, melted butter, honey, and vanilla essence in a separate basin.
3. Mix until just mixed, and pour the wet components into the dry ingredients.
4. Grease a non-stick skillet or griddle with butter or oil and heat it over medium heat.
5. For each pancake, add 1/4 cup of batter to the skillet.
6. Fry until surface bubbles appear, then turn and continue cooking until both sides are golden brown.
7. If preferred, garnish with fresh fruit and a sprinkle of maple syrup or honey before serving.

Value Nutritionally:

- ☐ About 300 calories are included in each serving (2 pancakes).

- ☐ 8 grams of protein

- ☐ Grams of carbohydrates: 45

- ☐ Ten grams of fat

- ☐ Five grams of fiber

Duration of Preparation:

Twenty minutes

1.7 Berries and Yogurt on Waffles

For an extra nutritional boost, try making waffles with whole-wheat flour for a delicious breakfast option. For the ideal harmony of tastes and textures, top them with yogurt and fresh berries.

Ingredients:

1. One cup of whole-wheat flour
2. One-third tsp baking powder
3. Half a teaspoon of salt

4. One cup of milk (vegan or dairy)
5. One big egg
6. Two teaspoons of oil or melted butter
7. One tablespoon of maple syrup or honey (optional)
8. One teaspoon of optional vanilla extract
9. Topping: fresh berries
10. half a cup of Greek yogurt

Preparation:

- Warm up your waffle maker.

- Combine the whole-wheat flour, baking powder, and salt in a large basin.

- Mix the milk, egg, melted butter, honey, and vanilla essence in a separate basin.

- Mix until just mixed, and pour the wet components into the dry ingredients.

- Transfer the batter to the waffle iron that has been warmed, and cook it as directed by the maker until it becomes golden brown.

- Serve with a dollop of Greek yogurt and fresh berries on top.

Value Nutritionally:

☐ Around 350 calories per serving.

☐ 12 grams of protein

☐ Fifty grams of carbs

- ☐ 12 grams of fat

- ☐ Six grams of fiber

Duration of Preparation:

Twenty minutes

1.8 Milk, yogurt, and fruit overnight oats

The pinnacle of ease and nourishment is achieved with overnight oats. Made the night before, these nutrient-dense, high-protein, fiber-containing foods are ready to enjoy in the morning.

Ingredients:
- Half a cup of rolled oats
- Half a cup of milk (vegan or dairy)
- half a cup of Greek yogurt
- One tablespoon of optional chia seeds
- half a cup of mixed frozen or fresh fruit
- One tablespoon of maple syrup or honey (optional)

Ingredients

- Combine the rolled oats, milk, Greek yogurt, and chia seeds in an airtight jar or mason jar.
- Mix well to blend.

- Add mixed fruit on top.
- Refrigerate overnight with a cover on.
- In the morning, mix the oats and adjust the consistency with more milk if necessary.
- Before serving, drizzle with maple syrup or honey, if preferred.

Value Nutritionally:

- Around 350 calories per serving.
- 15 grams of protein
- Grams of carbohydrates: 55
- 8 grams of fat
- 8 grams of fiber

Duration of Preparation:

Five minutes (plus refrigerated overnight)

1.9 Eggs, beans, and veggies in breakfast burritos

A portable breakfast burrito is a great way to pack a lot of nutrients into a little meal. Rich in fiber, protein, and vitamins, they make a satisfying breakfast or a quick snack.

Ingredients:

- Two big eggs
- 1/4 cup washed and drained black beans
- 1/4 cup of bell peppers, chopped
- one-fourth cup of chopped tomatoes
- 1/4 cup of shredded cheese, either cheddar or another kind
- One tablespoon of butter or olive oil
- Two tacos made using whole-wheat
- Slices of avocado and salsa (optional)

Preparation:

1. Whisk the eggs with a dash of salt and pepper in a small bowl.
2. Put butter or olive oil in a pan and heat it to medium.

3. Add the tomatoes and bell peppers and cook for 3–4 minutes, or until the vegetables are tender.
4. When the black beans are well heated, add them and cook.
5. Add the eggs and scramble them until they are cooked through.
6. Spoon half of the egg mixture onto each tortilla.
7. Add some cheese shreds on top.
8. To keep the filling in place, fold the tortillas in half as you roll them up.
9. If desired, garnish with avocado slices and salsa.

Value Nutritionally:

☐ Around 400 calories per serving.

- ☐ 20 grams of protein

- ☐ Grams of carbohydrates: 45

- ☐ 15 grams of fat

- ☐ Ten grams of fiber

Duration of Preparation:

fifteen minutes

2.0 Fruit and Nut Chia Seed Pudding

First of all, Chia seed pudding is a high-protein, high-fiber, and nutrient-dense breakfast dish that may be prepared ahead of time. For a filling supper, this creamy pudding tastes great with fresh fruit and crunchy almonds.

Ingredients

- One-fourth cup of chia seeds
- One cup of milk (vegan or dairy)
- Half a teaspoon of optional vanilla essence
- One tablespoon of maple syrup or honey (optional)
- half a cup of assorted fresh fruit
- one-fourth cup of mixed nuts

Preparation:

1. Chia seeds, milk, vanilla essence, honey, or maple syrup should all be combined in a dish or container.
2. For the chia seeds to be dispersed uniformly, give it a good stir.
3. For at least four hours, ideally overnight, cover and chill.
4. To break up any clumps, stir the pudding in the morning.
5. Before serving, scatter some mixed fresh fruit and nuts on top.

Value Nutritionally:

☐ Around 300 calories per serving.

☐ 10 grams of protein

☐ thirty grams of carbs

☐ 15 grams of fat

☐ 12 grams of fiber

Duration of Preparation:

Five minutes (plus refrigerated overnight)

To accommodate diverse palates and dietary requirements, these breakfast dishes provide an array of tastes, textures, and nutritional advantages. You may have a healthy and fulfilling start to the day by including these meals in your regimen.

Chapter 2: Lunch

A healthy lunch gives you the energy you need to go through the afternoon. Proteins, carbs, and good fats should all be included in moderation to keep you full and concentrated. This chapter explores 10 delicious lunch meals that are both simple to make and packed with nutrients. You may eat these meals at home, at work, or in a lunchbox to stay full and energetic.

2.1 Whole-wheat bread Sandwiches with Tuna Salad

Sandwiches with tuna salad are a classic lunch choice. This dish is satiating and nourishing because it combines the fiber of whole-wheat bread with the rich protein of tuna. It's ideal for a fast lunch at home or a well-packed lunch in the office or classroom.

Ingredients:

- One can (5 oz) of drained tuna
- Mayonnaise, two tablespoons
- One spoonful of mustard dijon
- One celery stalk cut finely
- 1/4 cup of coarsely chopped red onion
- One tablespoon of freshly squeezed lemon juice
- To taste, add salt and pepper.
- Four whole-wheat slices of bread
- Leaves from lettuce (optional)
- Slices of tomato (optional)

Preparation:

1. The drained tuna, mayonnaise, Dijon mustard, red onion, celery, and lemon juice should all be combined in a bowl. Blend well.
2. To taste, add salt and pepper for seasoning.

3. If preferred, toast the pieces of whole-wheat bread.
4. Evenly divide the tuna salad between the two pieces of bread.
5. Add lettuce leaves and, if using, tomato slices on top.
6. To make sandwiches, place the remaining bread pieces on top.
7. After cutting in half, serve.

Nutritionally Value:

- ☐ 350 calories per sandwich; 25 grams of protein
- ☐ thirty grams of carbs
- ☐ 15 grams of fat
- ☐ Five grams of fiber

Duration of Preparation:

Ten minutes

2.2 Hummus-topped chicken nuggets

Both children and adults love chicken nuggets. They provide a well-balanced supper with protein and good fats when combined with hummus. This homemade version tastes just as good and is healthier than the fast-food equivalent.

Ingredients:

- Two skinless, boneless chicken breasts, sliced into pieces the size of nuggets
- One cup of breadcrumbs made with whole wheat
- Grated Parmesan cheese, half a cup
- one tsp powdered garlic
- One tsp powdered onion
- To taste, add salt and pepper.
- two beaten eggs
- One cup of hummus, homemade or from the store

Preparation:

1. Adjust the oven temperature to 400°F (200°C) and place parchment paper on a baking pan.
2. Mix the breadcrumbs, Parmesan cheese, onion and

garlic powders, salt, and pepper in a bowl.

3. Coat each piece of chicken in the breadcrumb mixture after dipping it into the beaten eggs.

4. Arrange the coated chicken nuggets onto the ready baking sheet.

5. Bake the nuggets for 15 to 20 minutes, or until they are cooked through and golden brown.

6. Present the chicken nuggets beside a dish of hummus for dunks.

Nutritionally Value:

☐ Around 400 calories per serving.
☐ 30 grams of protein
☐ thirty grams of carbs
☐ 15 grams of fat

☐ Five grams of fiber

Duration of Preparation:

Thirty minutes

2.3 Crackers Made with Whole Wheat and Lentils Soup

For a filling and healthy lunch, lentil soup is a great option. This soup is packed with critical vitamins, protein, and fiber. It tastes great with whole-wheat crackers for extra crunch and fiber.

Ingredients:

- one cup of washed dry lentils
- One tablespoon of olive oil
- One onion, chopped; two carrots; two celery stalks; diced; three minced garlic cloves
- One teaspoon of cumin powder
- A single tsp of dried thyme
- Six cups veggie broth and one bay leaf
- To taste, add salt and pepper.
- 1/4 cup fresh parsley, chopped (optional)
- Serve with whole-wheat crackers

Preparation:

1. Heat the olive oil in a big saucepan over medium heat.
2. Stir in the celery, carrots, and onion. Sauté the veggies for five to seven minutes, or until they are soft.
3. Add the bay leaf, thyme, cumin, and garlic. Simmer for two more minutes.
4. Add the veggie broth and lentils and stir.
5. After bringing to a boil, lower the heat, and simmer the lentils for 30 to 40 minutes, or until they are soft.
6. To taste, add salt and pepper for seasoning.
7. Take out the bay leaf and, if using, mix in some fresh parsley.
8. Warm-up and accompany with whole-wheat crackers.

Nutritionally Value:

- ☐ Around 300 calories per serving.
- ☐ 15 grams of protein
- ☐ Grams of carbohydrates: 45
- ☐ Six grams of fat
- ☐ 15 grams of fiber

Duration of Preparation:

Forty minutes

2.4 Quinoa Salad with Chickpeas and Vegetables

Quinoa salad is a healthy, adaptable recipe that tastes great both warm and cold. This recipe is a well-rounded and filling lunch choice since it has vibrant veggies and protein-rich chickpeas.

Ingredients:

- 1 cup washed quinoa and 2 cups water
- One can (15 oz) of washed and drained chickpeas; one cup of cherry tomatoes; one cucumber; one chopped red bell pepper;
- 1/4 cup of coarsely chopped red onion
- 1/4 cup of freshly chopped parsley
- 1/4 cup fresh mint, chopped (optional)
- Three teaspoons of olive oil

- two tsp freshly squeezed lemon juice

Preparation:
- To taste, add salt and pepper. Prepare
- Bring the water and quinoa to a boil in a medium-sized saucepan.
- Once the water has been absorbed and the quinoa is cooked, reduce heat to low, cover, and simmer for 15 minutes.
- Take off the heat and leave it covered for five minutes. Using a fork, fluff and let to cool.
- The cooked quinoa, chickpeas, cherry tomatoes, cucumber, red bell pepper, red onion, parsley, and mint, if used, should all be combined in a big bowl.

- Mix the lemon juice, olive oil, salt, and pepper in a small bowl.
- After adding the dressing, toss the quinoa salad to mix it well.
- Serve right now or store in the fridge for later.

Value Nutritionally:

- ☐ Around 350 calories per serving.
- ☐ 12 grams of protein
- ☐ Fifty grams of carbs
- ☐ 12 grams of fat
- ☐ Ten grams of fiber

Duration of Preparation:

Thirty minutes

2.5 Little Whole-Wheat Pizzas with Crust

A fun and adaptable lunch choice is a little pizza. Whole-wheat crusts are high in fiber and nutrients, and the variety of toppings available encourages experimentation and countless taste combinations.

Ingredients:

- Four tiny pizza crusts or whole-wheat pita breads
- One cup of marinara sauce

- 1/2 cup of mozzarella cheese, shredded
- Half a cup of sliced mushrooms
- Sliced bell peppers, half a cup
- 1/4 cup of black olives, sliced
- 1/4 cup fresh basil, chopped (optional)
- To taste, add salt and pepper.

Preparation:
- Set oven temperature to 400°F, or 200°C.
- Arrange the tiny pizza crusts or whole-wheat pitas onto a baking sheet.
- Cover each crust with a thin coating of marinara sauce.
- Add some shredded mozzarella cheese on top.
- Add the bell peppers, mushrooms, and black olives that you like on top.

- Add pepper and salt for seasoning.
- Bake for 10 to 12 minutes, or until the cheese is bubbling and melted, in a preheated oven.
- Take out of the oven and, if desired, top with freshly chopped basil.
- Warm up the food.

Value Nutritionally:

- About 300 calories per mini pizza; 15 grams of protein
- Grams of carbohydrates: 35
- 12 grams of fat
- Six grams of fiber

Duration of Preparation:

Twenty minutes

2.6 Brown rice with bean and cheese burritos

A filling and substantial lunch choice is bean and cheese burritos. The addition of whole grains and fiber from the brown rice makes this dish not only tasty but also nutrient-dense.

Ingredients:

- One cup of brown rice, cooked
- One can (15 oz) washed and drained black beans

- One cup of shredded cheese, either Monterey Jack or cheddar
- half a cup of salsa
- Four tacos made with whole wheat
- One sliced avocado (optional)
- 1/4 cup fresh cilantro, chopped (optional)

Preparation:

1. The cooked brown rice, black beans, salsa, and shredded cheese should all be combined in a big dish.
2. Spoon about 1/4 of the mixture into the middle of a tortilla that has been placed on a level surface.
3. To encompass the filling, fold in the sides and wrap up the tortilla.

4. Continue this process with the remaining tortillas and filling.
5. A nonstick skillet should be heated to medium heat.
6. Seam-side down, place the burritos in the pan and cook for 2 to 3 minutes on each side, or until thoroughly cooked and golden brown.
7. If preferred, garnish with fresh cilantro and avocado slices.

Value Nutritionally:

- ☐ About 400 calories per tortilla.
- ☐ 15 grams of protein
- ☐ Fifty grams of carbs
- ☐ 15 grams of fat
- ☐ Ten grams of fiber

Duration of Preparation:

Twenty minutes

2.7 Pasta leftovers paired with vegetables and marinara sauce

A fast and easy lunch choice is leftover spaghetti. The recipe is revitalized by the addition of fresh veggies and marinara sauce, offering a well-balanced supper high in fiber, carbs, and vitamins.

Ingredients:

- two cups of cooked pasta, any kind
- One cup of marinara sauce
- Half a cup of sliced mushrooms
- half a cup of chopped zucchini
- Diced bell peppers, 1/2 cup
- One tablespoon of olive oil
- 1/4 cup of optionally grated Parmesan cheese
- To taste, add salt and pepper.

Preparation:

1. Heat the olive oil in a big skillet over medium heat.
2. Add the bell peppers, zucchini, and mushrooms. Sauté for five to seven minutes, or until soft.
3. To the skillet, add the cooked pasta and marinara sauce. Mix everything.

4. Simmer for approximately 5 minutes, or until the pasta is well warm.
5. To taste, add salt and pepper for seasoning.
6. If preferred, top with grated Parmesan cheese and serve.

Value Nutritionally:

- ☐ Around 350 calories per serving.
- ☐ 10 grams of protein
- ☐ Grams of carbohydrates: 55
- ☐ Ten grams of fat
- ☐ 7 grams of fiber

Duration of Preparation:

fifteen minutes

2.8 Vegetable-Crusted Chicken Wraps

A light yet satisfying lunch choice is grill-cooked chicken wraps. This dish, which combines fresh veggies and lean protein in a whole-wheat wrap, is filling and healthful.

Ingredients:

- Two skinless and boneless chicken breasts
- One tablespoon of olive oil
- To taste, add salt and pepper.
- one tsp powdered garlic

- One tsp of paprika
- Four tacos made with whole wheat
- one cup of mixed greens
- half a cup of carrots, shredded
- Half a cup of cucumbers, sliced
- 1/4 cup of red onions, cut into slices
- 1/4 cup hummus (may be omitted)

Preparation:

1. Set the grill's temperature to medium-high.
- Season the chicken breasts with paprika, garlic powder, salt, and pepper after brushing them with olive oil.
- Cook the chicken on the grill for 6 to 8 minutes on each side, or until done.

- Take off of the grill, let it rest for five minutes, then thinly slice.
- After laying the whole-wheat tortillas flat, drizzle each one with a little amount of hummus, if using.
- On the tortillas, arrange the grilled chicken pieces, red onions, sliced cucumbers, mixed greens, and shredded carrots.
- To keep the filling in place, fold the tortillas in half as you roll them up.
- Serve right away.

Value Nutritionally:

- Around 350 calories per wrap.
- 25 grams of protein
- thirty grams of carbs
- 12 grams of fat

- Five grams of fiber

Duration of Preparation:

Twenty minutes

2.9 Vegetable and Hummus Pitas

A quick and healthful lunch alternative is these pitas with vegetables and hummus. This dish is full of fresh veggies and creamy hummus. It's also high in fiber, vitamins, and good fats, which make it a satisfying and healthful lunch.

Ingredients:

- Four pockets made with whole wheat
- One cup of hummus, homemade or from the store
- One cup of finely chopped lettuce
- half a cup of carrots, shredded
- Half a cup of cucumbers, sliced
- Sliced bell peppers, half a cup
- 1/4 cup of red onions, cut into slices
- 1/4 cup of feta cheese, crumbled (optional)

Preparation:

1. To make two pockets from each pita, cut the pockets in half.
2. Put a good dollop of hummus into each pita pocket.
3. Place shredded lettuce, bell peppers, cucumbers, carrots, and red onions into the pita pockets.
4. If using, top with crumbled feta cheese.
5. Serve right away.

Value Nutritionally:

- ☐ Three hundred calories a pita pocket
- ☐ 10 grams of protein
- ☐ forty grams of carbs
- ☐ Ten grams of fat
- ☐ 8 grams of fiber
- ☐ Duration of Preparation:

Ten minutes

3.0 Tuna Salad with Vegetables and Crackers

A simple but very filling lunch choice is tuna salad with crackers and veggies. This balanced dish of protein, fiber, and healthy fats is fast and simple to make, making it ideal for a picnic or quick lunch.

Ingredients:

- One can (5 oz) of drained tuna
- Mayonnaise, two tablespoons
- One spoonful of mustard dijon
- One celery stalk cut finely
- 1/4 cup of coarsely chopped red onion
- One tablespoon of freshly squeezed lemon juice
- To taste, add salt and pepper.
- Whole-grain crackers
- a variety of fresh veggies, including bell pepper strips, cucumber slices, and carrot sticks

Preparation:

1. The drained tuna, mayonnaise, Dijon mustard, red onion, celery, and lemon juice should all be combined in a bowl. Blend well.

2. To taste, add salt and pepper for seasoning.
3. Present the tuna salad with a variety of fresh veggies and whole-wheat crackers.

Value Nutritionally:

- ☐ Around 300 calories per serving.
- ☐ 20 grams of protein
- ☐ gram of carbohydrates: 25
- ☐ 12 grams of fat
- ☐ Five grams of fiber

Duration of Preparation:

Ten minutes

Chapter 3: Dinner

Dinner is the last meal of the day, allowing you to unwind and savor a full meal. A balanced diet that includes plenty of veggies, healthy grains, and lean meats is crucial. This chapter features 10 delicious and healthful supper dishes that are all meant to be simple to make and very fulfilling.

3.1 Green beans and potatoes with roasted chicken

A traditional dish of soft green beans, crunchy potatoes, and juicy chicken is roasted chicken with potatoes and green beans. This balanced supper includes veggies, carbs, and protein to make it a full meal.

Ingredients:

- Four skin-on, bone-in chicken thighs
- One pound of halved baby potatoes and one pound of trimmed green beans
- Three teaspoons of olive oil
- four minced garlic cloves
- A single tsp of dried thyme
- One tsp of dehydrated rosemary
- To taste, add salt and pepper.
- slices of lemon to serve (optional)

Preparation:

1. Set the oven temperature to 425°F (220°C).
2. Combine the potatoes, thyme, rosemary, half of the minced garlic, 1 tablespoon olive oil, salt, and pepper in a big bowl.

Arrange them evenly on a baking tray.

3. Toss the green beans with the remaining garlic, 1 tablespoon olive oil, salt, and pepper in the same bowl. Put aside.

4. Season the chicken thighs with salt, pepper, and the remaining olive oil. Transfer them to the top of the baking sheet's potatoes.

5. Roast for 30 minutes in the preheated oven.

6. When the chicken is well cooked and the potatoes are golden brown, add the green beans to the oven sheet and continue to roast for a further fifteen minutes.

7. If preferred, serve hot with lemon slices on the side.

Value Nutritionally:

- ☐ Each dish has around 450 calories.
- ☐ 30 grams of protein
- ☐ Grams of carbohydrates: 35
- ☐ 20 grams of fat
- ☐ Six grams of fiber

Duration of Preparation:

Forty minutes

3.2 Sweet Potato Fries and Salmon Burgers

A tasty and wholesome supper option is salmon burgers with sweet potato fries. Omega-3 fatty acids are abundant in salmon, and it's a wonderful source of vitamins and fiber when paired with sweet potatoes.

Ingredients:

- ❖ Regarding the Salmon Burgers:

- ❖ One pound of fresh salmon with the skin removed and cut coarsely
- ❖ One-fourth cup of breadcrumbs
- ❖ One beaten egg
- ❖ Two tablespoons of red onion cut finely, and two teaspoons of freshly chopped parsley
- ❖ One spoonful of mustard dijon
- ❖ To taste, add salt and pepper.
- ❖ One tablespoon of olive oil

- ❖ For the Fries with Sweet Potatoes:

- ❖ Peel and chop two big sweet potatoes into fries.
- ❖ Two tsp olive oil
- ❖ One tsp of paprika
- ❖ half a teaspoon of powdered garlic
- ❖ To taste, add salt and pepper.

Preparation:

1. Set the oven temperature to 425°F (220°C). Use parchment paper to line a baking sheet.
2. Combine the sweet potato fries, olive oil, paprika, garlic powder, salt, and pepper in a big bowl. Arrange them on the prepared baking sheet in a single layer.

3. Bake the sweet potatoes for 25 to 30 minutes, rotating them halfway through, or until they are crispy and have a golden brown color.

4. Make the salmon burgers while the fries are baking. Mix the breadcrumbs, beaten egg, red onion, parsley, Dijon mustard, salt, and pepper in a dish with the diced salmon. Toss to blend thoroughly.

5. Create four patties out of the mixture.

6. One tablespoon of olive oil is heated over medium heat in a big skillet. The salmon patties should be cooked through and golden brown after 4–5 minutes on each side.

7. Present the salmon patties with sweet potato fries.

Value Nutritionally:

- ☐ 500 calories or so per dish.
- ☐ 30 grams of protein
- ☐ Fifty grams of carbs
- ☐ 20 grams of fat
- ☐ 8 grams of fiber

Duration of Preparation:

Forty minutes

3.3 Brown rice with veggie chili

For a nice evening, vegetarian chili is a filling and healthy dish that tastes great. It's a fantastic source of fiber and protein since it's loaded with beans, veggies, and spices. By serving it over brown rice, the dish incorporates entire grains.

Ingredients:

- One tablespoon of olive oil
- one sliced onion
- Two sliced bell peppers and three minced garlic cloves
- One chopped zucchini
- One cup of fresh or frozen corn kernels
- One can (15 oz) of rinsed and drained black beans
- One can (15 oz) of washed and drained kidney beans
- One 28-oz can of chopped tomatoes
- TWO TABLEspoONS tomato paste

- two tsp of chili powder
- One teaspoon of cumin powder
- One tsp of paprika
- To taste, add salt and pepper.
- Two cups cooked brown rice and one cup vegetable broth
- Fresh cilantro chopped (optional) for garnish

Preparation:

1. Heat the olive oil in a big saucepan over medium heat.
2. When the onions and bell peppers are tender, add them and sauté for approximately five minutes.
3. After adding the garlic, heat it for one more minute.
4. Add the chopped tomatoes, chili powder, cumin, paprika, black beans, kidney beans,

corn, zucchini, and salt and pepper.

5. After adding the veggie broth, bring it to a boil.
6. Simmer for thirty minutes over low heat, stirring now and again.
7. If preferred, top the cooked brown rice with chopped fresh cilantro before serving the chili.

Value Nutritionally:

☐ Around 400 calories per serving.
☐ 15 grams of protein
☐ 70 grams of carbohydrates
☐ 8 grams of fat
☐ 15 grams of fiber

Duration of Preparation:

Forty-five minutes

3.4 Pasta with Vegetables and Marinara Sauce

A simple yet tasty supper is pasta with veggies and marinara sauce. While a variety of veggies give vitamins and minerals to the meal, whole-wheat pasta ups the fiber content.

Ingredients:

- Eight ounces of whole-wheat pasta
- One tablespoon of olive oil
- One sliced onion and two minced garlic cloves
- One chopped zucchini and one sliced bell pepper
- One cup of sliced mushrooms
- One 28-oz can of crushed tomatoes
- One tsp of dried basil
- One tsp of dehydrated oregano
- To taste, add salt and pepper.
- 1/4 cup of optionally grated Parmesan cheese
- Garnish with fresh basil leaves (optional).

Preparation:

1. Follow the directions on the box to cook the pasta. After draining, put it away.

2. Heat the olive oil in a big skillet over medium heat.
3. Add the onion and garlic, and cook for approximately two minutes, or until fragrant.
4. Add the mushrooms, bell pepper, and zucchini. Simmer the veggies for 5 to 7 minutes, or until they are soft.
5. Add the dried oregano, dry basil, dried tomatoes, salt, and pepper and stir. Simmer for ten minutes.
6. When the pasta is done, add it to the pan and toss to cover with sauce.
7. If preferred, top with freshly chopped basil leaves and grated Parmesan cheese.

Value Nutritionally:

- ☐ Around 350 calories per serving.
- ☐ 12 grams of protein
- ☐ Grams of carbohydrates: 65
- ☐ Six grams of fat
- ☐ Ten grams of fiber

Duration of Preparation:

Thirty minutes

3.5 Fish on the Grill with Herbs and Lemon

A light and healthful supper choice is grilled fish with lemon and herbs. Omega-3 fatty acids and lean protein are both abundant in fish. This dish is tasty and easy to put together for a fast midweek supper.

Preparation:

- Four filets of fish, preferably tilapia, cod, or salmon
- Two tsp olive oil
- One lemon's juice
- two minced garlic cloves
- One tablespoon of freshly chopped parsley
- One tablespoon of freshly chopped dill, optional
- To taste, add salt and pepper.
- slices of lemon for serving

Preparation:

1. Set the grill's temperature to medium-high.
2. Olive oil, lemon juice, garlic, parsley, dill, salt, and pepper should all be combined in a small bowl.
3. Apply the olive oil mixture to the fish filets.
4. When the salmon is opaque and flakes easily with a fork, place the filets on the grill and cook for 4–5 minutes on each side.
5. Accompany with slices of lemon.

Value Nutritionally:

- ☐ Around 300 calories per serving.
- ☐ 25 grams of protein
- ☐ Three grams of carbs
- ☐ 20 grams of fat

☐ One gram of fiber

Duration of Preparation:

Twenty minutes

3.6 Brown rice stir-fried with chicken

A simple and wholesome supper option is stir-fried chicken over brown rice. Lean chicken, vibrant veggies, and whole-grain rice combine to create a tasty and well-balanced dinner.

Ingredients:

- Two tsp soy sauce
- One tsp of hoisin sauce
- One-tsp rice vinegar
- One tsp of sesame oil
- One tablespoon of olive oil
- One pound of sliced, skinless, boneless chicken breasts
- two minced garlic cloves
- One tablespoon of freshly grated ginger
- One sliced bell pepper
- one cup florets of broccoli
- One cup of carrots, sliced
- two cups of brown rice, cooked
- chopped green onions (optional) as a garnish
- Add a garnish of sesame seeds (optional).

Preparation:

1. Mix the rice vinegar, sesame oil, hoisin sauce, and soy sauce in a small bowl. Put aside.
2. In a large skillet or wok, heat the olive oil over medium-high heat.
3. After adding the chicken strips, heat for 5 to 7 minutes, or until browned and cooked through.
4. Cook for an additional minute after adding the ginger and garlic to the skillet.
5. To the skillet, add the bell pepper, carrots, and broccoli. Cook for approximately 5 minutes, or until the veggies are crisp-tender.
6. Over the chicken and veggies in the pan, pour the sauce. Add a few more minutes of cooking and stir to ensure even coating.

- After the brown rice is done, serve the stir-fry.
- If preferred, garnish with sesame seeds and chopped green onions.

Value Nutritionally:

- ☐ Around 400 calories per serving.
- ☐ 30 grams of protein
- ☐ forty grams of carbs
- ☐ 12 grams of fat
- ☐ Six grams of fiber

Duration of Preparation:

Thirty minutes

3.7 Whole-Wheat Tortillas with Lentil Tacos

Whole-wheat tortillas paired with lentil tacos provide a filling and healthy supper choice. Since lentils are a fantastic plant-based source of fiber and protein, they make a perfect meat substitute for tacos.

Ingredients:

- one cup of washed dry lentils
- Two cups of veggie broth and one spoonful of olive oil

- one sliced onion
- two minced garlic cloves
- One tablespoon of powdered chilies
- One teaspoon of cumin powder
- Half a teaspoon of paprika
- To taste, add salt and pepper.
- Eight tortillas made with whole wheat
- Add-ons: Greek yogurt (optional), salsa, chopped avocado, diced tomatoes, and shredded lettuce

Preparation:

1. Combine the lentils and vegetable broth in a medium-sized pot. Once the lentils are soft and the liquid has been absorbed, bring to a boil, lower the heat, and simmer for 20 to 25 minutes.

2. Meanwhile, place a skillet over medium heat with the olive oil.
3. Add the onion and garlic and cook for approximately 5 minutes, or until softened.
4. Add the paprika, cumin, chili powder, salt, and pepper and stir. Simmer for a further minute.
5. Stir the cooked lentils into the skillet after adding them.
6. The whole-wheat tortillas may be reheated in a microwave or dry skillet.
7. After spooning the lentil mixture onto the tortillas, garnish with Greek yogurt, chopped avocado, sliced tomatoes, diced lettuce, and salsa, if preferred.
8. Serve right away.

Value Nutritionally:

- ☐ Around 350 calories per serving.
- ☐ 15 grams of protein
- ☐ Grams of carbohydrates: 55
- ☐ 8 grams of fat
- ☐ 12 grams of fiber

Duration of Preparation:

Forty minutes

3.8 Shepherd's Pie with Sweet Potato Topping and Ground Turkey

A hearty and cozy supper is shepherd's pie with sweet potato topping and ground turkey. This healthy take on the traditional recipe combines nutrient-dense sweet potatoes with lean ground turkey to create a filling supper.

Ingredients:

- One tablespoon of olive oil
- One chopped onion and two diced carrots
- two minced garlic cloves
- One pound of turkey, ground
- One spoonful of pasted tomatoes
- One cup of frozen peas
- One cup of broth made with vegetables
- To taste, add salt and pepper.

- Regarding the Sweet Potato Garnish:

- Two big sweet potatoes, chopped and skinned
- two tsp butter
- one-fourth cup milk
- To taste, add salt and pepper.

Preparation:

1. Turn the oven on to 375°F, or 190°C.
2. Heat the olive oil in a big skillet over medium heat.
3. Add the garlic, onion, and carrots. After around five minutes, sauté until softened.
4. Using a spoon, break up the ground turkey as you cook it until it becomes brown.
5. Add the frozen peas, vegetable broth, tomato paste, salt, and

pepper and stir. Simmer for ten minutes.

6. In the meantime, boil the sweet potatoes in diced form for approximately 15 minutes, or until they are cooked. Make sure to drain properly.

7. Sweet potatoes should be smoothed out by mashing them with butter, milk, salt, and pepper.

8. Spoon the mixture of turkey into a baking dish. Evenly distribute the mashed sweet potatoes on top.

9. Bake for 25 to 30 minutes in a preheated oven, or until the sweet potato topping is caramelized.

10. Warm up the food.

Value Nutritionally:

- ☐ Around 400 calories per serving.
- ☐ 25 grams of protein
- ☐ forty grams of carbs
- ☐ 15 grams of fat
- ☐ 8 grams of fiber

Duration of Preparation:

For sixty minutes

3.9 Soup with Vegetables and Beans Overview

Soup made with vegetables and beans is a filling and healthy supper choice. Tight with a bounty of veggies and full of protein from the beans, this soup is hearty and filling.

Ingredients:

- One tablespoon of olive oil
- One onion, chopped; two carrots; two celery stalks; two minced garlic cloves;
- One can (15 oz) chopped tomatoes
- 15 oz can; 4 cups vegetable broth washed and drained cannellini beans
- 1 cup finely chopped spinach or greens
- A single tsp of dried thyme
- One tsp of dehydrated oregano
- To taste, add salt and pepper.

Preparation:

1. Heat the olive oil in a big saucepan over medium heat.
2. Stir in the celery, carrots, and onion. After around five minutes, sauté until softened.
3. After adding the garlic, heat it for one more minute.
4. Add the chopped tomatoes, cannellini beans, vegetable broth, oregano, thyme, and season with salt and pepper.
5. The soup should be brought to a boil, then simmered for 20 to 25 minutes on low heat.
6. After adding the chopped spinach or kale, simmer for a further five minutes.
7. Modify the seasoning as needed.
8. Warm up the food.

Value Nutritionally:

- ☐ Around 250 calories per serving.
- ☐ 10 grams of protein
- ☐ Grams of carbohydrates: 35
- ☐ Six grams of fat
- ☐ Ten grams of fiber

Duration of Preparation:

Forty minutes

Chapter 4:
Appetizers

For youngsters, snacks are a crucial component of a balanced diet. They may help youngsters stay energetic and avoid being too hungry in between meals. Fruits, vegetables, nuts, seeds, yogurt, and other healthful and nutrient-dense ingredients are often included in Mediterranean snacks.

4.1 Berries, bananas, and apples

Fruit is a fantastic source of antioxidants, vitamins, and minerals. Additionally, it's a fantastic source of fiber, which helps maintain kids' feelings of fullness and satisfaction.

Components:

· One cup of berries; one banana; one apple

Getting ready:

1. wash the fruit.

2. Make slices out of the banana and apple.

3. Present the fruit in a bowl or on a platter.

Value nutritionally:

- 200 calories; 0 grams of fat
- Fifty grams of carbs
- Five grams of protein
- Ten grams of fiber

Five minutes were spent preparing.

4.2 Vegetables (cucumbers, carrots, and celery)

Vegetables are an excellent source of fiber, vitamins, and minerals. They're a fantastic kid-friendly snack choice since they're minimal in calories.

Components:

- One cup of sliced carrots
- One cup of sliced celery
- One cup of sliced cucumbers

Getting ready:

1. wash the veggies.
2. Trim and cut the cucumbers, celery, and carrots into sticks.
3. Present the veggies with a dip, such as guacamole or hummus, on a platter or in a bowl.

Value nutritionally:

- There are 100 calories.
- There are no grams of fat.
- 25 grams of carbohydrates

- Two grams of protein
- Five grams of fiber

Five minutes were spent preparing.

4.3 Seeds and Nuts

Nuts and seeds are excellent sources of fiber, protein, and beneficial fats. They're a fantastic source of minerals and vitamins as well.

Components:

- 1/4 cup pumpkin seeds; 1/4 cup walnuts; and 1/4 cup almonds

Getting ready:

1. In a dish, mix the nuts and seeds.

2. Transfer the seeds and nuts to a dish or platter.

Value nutritionally:

- 200 calories
- 15 grams of fat
- Grams of carbohydrates: 10
- 10 grams of protein
- Five grams of fiber

Two minutes were spent preparing.

4.4 Milk

Probiotics, or healthy bacteria that promote gut health, are present in yogurt and are a rich source of protein and calcium. It's a fantastic source of minerals and vitamins as well.

Components:

· A single cup of yogurt

Getting ready:

1. Use a dish or cup to serve the yogurt.
2. If preferred, sprinkle nuts, granola, or fruit on top of the yogurt.

Value nutritionally:

- 150 calories and 5 grams of fat
· 20 grams of carbohydrates; 10 grams of protein
· There are zero grams of fiber.

Two minutes were spent preparing.

4.5 Trail Mix

Kids may enjoy trail mix as a healthy and portable snack since it's high in nutrients. It's a wonderful source of fiber, protein, and beneficial fats.

Components:

· Half a cup of nuts, such as pecans, walnuts, or almonds
· Half a cup of seeds, such as flax, sunflower, or pumpkin seeds
· Half a cup of dried fruit, such as apricots, cranberries, or raisins

Getting ready:

1. In a dish, mix the nuts, seeds, and dried fruit.

2. Keep the trail mix sealed in a container.

Value nutritionally:

- 200 calories; 10 grams of fat
- 25 grams of carbohydrates
- 10 grams of protein
- Five grams of fiber

Five minutes were spent preparing.

4.6 Eggs Hard-Boiled

Eggs that have been hard-boiled are a fantastic source of healthful fats and protein. They're a fantastic source of minerals and vitamins as well.

Components:

· Six eggs

Getting ready:

1. Transfer the eggs into a saucepan in a single layer.
2. Pour cold water over the eggs.
3. Use high heat to bring the water to a boil.
4. After the water reaches a boil, cover the pan and turn off the heat.
5. Depending on how hard you want them to be, let the eggs stand in the boiling water for 10 to 12 minutes.
6. To halt the cooking process, take the eggs out of the boiling water and put them in a dish of cool water.
7. After peeling, serve the eggs whole or sliced.

Value nutritionally:

· There are 100 calories.

· Grams of fat: 5

One gram of carbohydrates and six grams of protein

· There are zero grams of fiber.

15 minutes were spent preparing.

4.7 Cottage Cheese

A wonderful source of calcium and protein is cottage cheese. It's a fantastic source of minerals and vitamins as well.

Components:

· One cup of cottage cheese

Getting ready:

1. Place the cottage cheese in a bowl for serving.
2. If preferred, sprinkle nuts, cereals, or fruit on top of the cottage cheese.

Value nutritionally:

- 150 calories, 5 grams of fat, and 10 grams of carbohydrates
· 25 grams of protein
· There are zero grams of fiber.

4.8 Popcorn cooked al dente

Two minutes were spent preparing.

Popcorn that has been air-popped is a whole-grain snack that is low in fat and calories. It's a wonderful source of fiber as well.

Components:

· Half a cup of popcorn kernels

Getting ready:

1. Fill an air popper with popcorn kernels.
2. Prepare the popcorn as directed by the manufacturer.
3. Use a bowl to serve the popcorn.

Value nutritionally:

· There are 100 calories.
· 20 grams of carbohydrates; 1 gram of fat; 3 grams of protein
· Five grams of fiber

Five minutes were spent preparing.

4.9 Hummus-topped Whole-Wheat Crackers

Kids may enjoy whole-wheat crackers with hummus as a snack since they're a healthy source of fiber, protein, and complex carbs.

Components:

Ten whole-wheat crackers and half a cup of hummus.

Getting ready:

1. Top the crackers with hummus.
2. Place the crackers in a dish or on a platter and serve with hummus.

Chapter 5: Sweet Treats

Desserts are a unique addition to every dinner, and children may particularly love them. Desserts from the Mediterranean region are usually cool and light, with plenty of fruit, almonds, and yogurt. The sweetness and nutrients in this mixture of foods are well-balanced.

5.1 Honey-Dried Fruit Salad

A traditional dessert that never fails to please children is fruit salad. It is rich in minerals, vitamins, and antioxidants.

Components:

· One cup of berries, such as raspberries, blueberries, or strawberries
· One cup of diced melon (honeydew or cantaloupe)
· 1/4 cup chopped nuts (almonds, walnuts, or pecans) · 1 cup chopped pineapple
· One tsp honey

Getting ready:

1. In a dish, mix the berries, melon, pineapple, almonds, and honey.
2. Toss to incorporate.
3. Use dishes or cups to serve the fruit salad.

Value nutritionally:

· 200 calories

- Grams of fat: 5
- Forty grams of carbohydrates
- Five grams of protein
- Five grams of fiber

Ten minutes were spent preparing.

5.2 Yogurt in Frozen Form

Delicious and healthful frozen yogurt may be substituted for ice cream. It's an excellent source of calcium and protein.

Components:

- One cup of plain yogurt
- 1/4 cup pureed fruit (such as raspberries, blueberries, or strawberries) · 1 tablespoon honey

Getting ready:

1. In a blender, combine the yogurt, pureed fruit, and honey.
2. Process until smooth.
3. Transfer the blend onto an ice cube tray or popsicle mold.
4. Freeze until solid, or for at least 4 hours.

Value nutritionally:

150 calories, 5 grams fat, 25 grams carbs, and 10 grams protein.
· There are zero grams of fiber.

15 minutes for preparation + freezing time

5.3 Cinnamon Apples Baked

A cozy and warming treat that is ideal for autumn and winter is baked apples. They're a fantastic source of vitamin C and fiber.

Components:

· 4 apples, 1/4 cup sugar, 1/4 cup water, and 1 teaspoon of ground cinnamon

Getting ready:

1. Set oven temperature to 350 degrees.
2. After cooking, put the apples in a baking dish.
3. In a dish, mix the water, cinnamon, and sugar.
4. Spoon the sugar mixture into the middle of each apple.
5. Bake the apples for thirty to forty minutes, or until they are soft.

Value nutritionally:

- 200 calories; 0 grams of fat
- Fifty grams of carbs
- Five grams of protein
- Ten grams of fiber

15 minutes for preparation + baking time

5.4 Cookies Made Whole-Wheat

Traditional cookies may be replaced with healthier options like whole-wheat cookies. Whole-wheat flour, a wonderful source of nutrients and fiber, is used to make them.

Components:

One cup whole-wheat flour; half a cup sugar; one egg; half a teaspoon baking soda; one-fourth teaspoon salt; one cup melted butter; one-fourth cup honey; and, optionally, half a cup chocolate chips

Getting ready:

1. Set oven temperature to 350 degrees.
2. Use parchment paper to line a baking sheet.
3. Combine the flour, sugar, baking soda, and salt in a medium-sized basin using a whisk.
4. Cream the butter and honey in another dish until the mixture is light and fluffy.
5. Add the egg and beat.

6. Combine the dry ingredients with the wet ones, mixing just until they are incorporated.

7. If desired, fold in the chocolate chips.

8. Transfer the dough onto the baking sheet that has been ready by rounding tablespoons.

9. Bake for ten to twelve minutes, or until golden brown around the edges.

Value nutritionally:

150 calories and 5 grams of fat
· 25 grams of carbohydrates
· Five grams of protein
· Five grams of fiber

20 minutes for preparation + baking time

5.5 Popsicles with Fruit

Fruit popsicles are a tasty and nutritious after-dinner treat. Yogurt and fruit puree, which are both excellent providers of vitamins and minerals, are used to make them.

Components:

· One cup yogurt; one cup fruit puree (strawberry, blueberry, or raspberry)
· One tablespoon of honey, if desired

Getting ready:

1. In a blender, combine the yogurt, fruit puree, and honey (if using).
2. Process until smooth.
3. Transfer the blend into ice cube trays or popsicle molds.

4. Freeze until solid, or for at least 4 hours.

Value nutritionally:

· There are 100 calories.
· There are no grams of fat.
20 grams of carbohydrates and 5 grams of protein
· Five grams of fiber

Ten minutes for preparation + freezing time

5.6 Fruit and Rice Pudding

Rice, milk, and sugar are the ingredients of this traditional delicacy, rice pudding. It's a fantastic source of protein and carbs.

Components:

• 1/4 cup sugar; 1/4 teaspoon ground cinnamon; 1/2 cup fruit (such as berries, bananas, or peaches); 1 cup white rice; 3 cups milk;

Getting ready:

1. Place the rice, milk, sugar, and cinnamon in a medium-sized pot.
2. Place over medium heat and bring to a boil.
3. Simmer the rice for 15 minutes, or until it is soft and the pudding has thickened, over low heat with a lid.
4. Turn off the heat and add the fruit.

Value nutritionally:

• 200 calories

- Grams of fat: 5
- 35 grams of carbohydrates
- 10 grams of protein
- Five grams of fiber

Thirty minutes were spent preparing.

5.7 Nice Cream Banana

A tasty and nutritious substitute for ice cream is a banana lovely cream. Frozen bananas and other healthful components like fruit and yogurt are used to make it.

Components:

- Two frozen bananas; one-fourth cup of yogurt; one tablespoon of optional honey; and half a cup of fruit (bananas, peaches, or berries).

Getting ready:

1. Fill a blender with the frozen bananas, yogurt, fruit, and honey (if using).
2. Process until smooth.
3. You may freeze it for later or serve it right now.

Value nutritionally:

150 calories and 5 grams of fat
· Thirty grams of carbohydrates
· 10 grams of protein
· Ten grams of fiber

Ten minutes were spent preparing.

5.8 Fruit and Granola Yogurt Parfaits

A stacked treat consisting of yogurt, fruit, and granola is called a yogurt parfait. They're an excellent source of fiber, carbs, and protein.

Components:

· A single cup of yogurt
· 1/4 cup granola; 1/2 cup fruit (bananas, peaches, or berries).

Getting ready:

1. Arrange the yogurt, fruit, and granola in a glass or container.
2. Continue layering until the jar or glass is filled.
3. Present right away.

Value nutritionally:

· 200 calories
· Grams of fat: 5
· Thirty grams of carbohydrates
· 10 grams of protein
· Five grams of fiber

Five minutes were spent preparing.

5.9 Handmade Fruit Leather

Made with fruit and a natural sweetener, homemade fruit leather is a tasty and healthful snack. It's an excellent source of fiber, vitamins, and minerals.

Components:

· Two pounds of fruit, preferably blueberries, raspberries, or strawberries
· One-fourth cup of maple syrup or honey

Getting ready:

1. Set oven temperature to 200 degrees F.
2. Use parchment paper to line a baking sheet.
3. Blend the fruit with the honey or maple syrup in a blender.
4. Process until smooth.
5. Transfer the batter to the ready baking sheet.
6. Evenly distribute the ingredients into a thin layer.
7. Bake the fruit leather for four to six hours, or until it becomes dry and leathery.

8. Before slicing the fruit leather into strips, let it cool fully.

Value nutritionally:

· There are 100 calories.
· There are no grams of fat.
· 25 grams of carbohydrates
· Two grams of protein
· Five grams of fiber

15 minutes for preparation + baking time

6.0 Fruit and Dark Chocolate

Fruit with dark chocolate makes a filling and healthful snack or dessert. It's a wonderful source of fiber, minerals, and antioxidants.

Components:

· One ounce of dark chocolate (at least 70% cocoa)
· Half a cup of fruit, preferably peaches, bananas, or berries

Getting ready:

1. Split the chocolate into tiny fragments.
2. Put the chocolate chunks in a small dish and heat in the microwave for 30 seconds, or just long enough to melt the chocolate.
3. Suck the fruit into the chocolate that has melted.
4. Transfer the fruit wrapped in chocolate to a dish or piece of parchment paper.

5. Place in the refrigerator until the chocolate has set, at least 30 minutes.

Value nutritionally:

150 calories and 10 grams of fat
20 grams of carbohydrates and 5 grams of protein
· Five grams of fiber

15 minutes for preparation + additional time for refrigeration

Chapter 6: Children's Help-Made Recipes

Teaching children to cook and eat healthily is a terrific way to include them in the kitchen. The entire family may enjoy and strengthen their bonds via it as well. These two dishes are ideal for children to assist in making:

6.1 Smoothie with Fruit and Vegetables

Smoothies made with fruits and vegetables are a fast and simple method to consume a variety of fruits and vegetables. They're also a fantastic way to finish up leftover veggies and fruit.

Components:

· One cup of fruit (bananas, peaches, or berries); one cup of veggies (carrots, spinach, or kale); one cup of yogurt
· 1 tablespoon honey (optional) · 1/2 cup milk

Getting ready:

Children may assist with:

preparing the fruit and vegetables by washing and cutting them; adding the ingredients to the blender; and pressing the button to start blending the smoothie

Value nutritionally:

· 250 calories

- Grams of fat: 5
- Forty grams of carbohydrates
- 15 grams of protein
- Five grams of fiber

Five minutes were spent preparing.

6.2 Little Pizzas

A simple and enjoyable method to include youngsters in the kitchen is via little pizzas. You may make them with whichever toppings your kids choose.

Components:

· One package (fourteen ounces) of premade pizza dough; one cup of shredded mozzarella cheese; half a cup of pizza sauce; and any desired toppings (pepperoni, sausage, veggies, or fruit).

Getting ready:

Children may assist with:

The steps involved in making pizza include rolling out the dough, spreading the sauce, adding cheese and toppings, and baking the pizza.

Value nutritionally:

· 250 calories
· 30 grams of carbohydrates; 10 grams of fat
· 15 grams of protein
· Five grams of fiber

15 minutes for preparation + baking time

A tasty and nutritious salad that's ideal for a light supper or lunch is chickpea salad. Vegetables, chickpeas, and a basic dressing are the ingredients.

Components:

· 1/2 cup chopped cucumber; 1/2 cup chopped red onion; 1/2 cup chopped celery; 1/4 cup chopped parsley; 1/4 cup olive oil; 1/4 cup lemon juice; 1 teaspoon dried oregano; 1/2 teaspoon salt; 1/4 teaspoon black pepper; and 1 can (15 ounces) washed and drained chickpeas

Getting ready:

Children may assist with:

Pulling the chickpeas and rinsing them; chopping the veggies; whisking the vinaigrette; and combining all the components

Value nutritionally:

- 250 calories
- Ten grams of fat
- Thirty grams of carbohydrates
- 15 grams of protein
- Ten grams of fiber

15 minutes were spent preparing.

6.4 Yogurt Bark

Fruit and yogurt combine to create the delectable and healthful treat known as yogurt bark. It's a fantastic way to finish up leftover fruit and yogurt.

Components:

· A single cup of yogurt
· Half a cup of chopped fruit (bananas, peaches, or berries).

Getting ready:

Children may assist with:

The yogurt may be spread out on a baking sheet, fruit can be sprinkled on top, and the yogurt bark can be frozen.

Value nutritionally:

150 calories and 5 grams of fat
· 25 grams of carbohydrates
· 10 grams of protein

· Five grams of fiber

15 minutes for preparation + freezing time

6.5 Personalized Granola

Made with oats, nuts, and seeds, homemade granola is a tasty and nutritious breakfast or snack. It's a fantastic way to use up nuts and leftover oats.

Components:

Two cups of rolled oats; one cup chopped nuts (almonds, walnuts, or pecans); one cup chopped seeds (sunflower, pumpkin, or flax seeds); half a cup honey; one-fourth cup olive oil; one-half teaspoon powder cinnamon; one-half teaspoon vanilla essence; and one-fourth teaspoon salt

Getting ready:

Children may assist with:

Spreading the granola on the baking sheet, measuring the ingredients, whisking them together, and baking the granola

Value nutritionally:

- 250 calories
- Ten grams of fat
- Thirty grams of carbohydrates
- 15 grams of protein
- Ten grams of fiber

15 minutes for preparation + baking time

Chapter 7: Parental Advice

It might be difficult to convince children to eat healthily, but it's crucial to realize that you're not doing this alone. Parents face this problem in large numbers. The good news is that there are many ways you can encourage your children to eat healthily.

7.1 How to Inspire Children to Eat Healthily

• Involve children in culinary activities. Children tend to consume meals that they have assisted in preparing more often. Allow children to assist you with basic chores like stirring, measuring, and cleaning fruits and veggies.

· Incorporate enjoyment with eating nutritious meals. Use cookie cutters to cut fruits and vegetables into interesting shapes, and produce vibrant fruit and vegetable plates.

· Provide wholesome options for each meal and snack. Offer more than simply bad food because it's convenient. Ensure that your children always have access to wholesome alternatives.

· Set an example for others. Children pick up knowledge from the elders in their lives. You must eat healthily yourself if you want your children to as well.

· Refrain from making youngsters eat nutritious meals. They will just get more resistant as a result. Rather, concentrate on making nutritious meals enticing and easily available.

7.2 Mediterranean Diet Meal Planning

Planning meals is a crucial component of any healthy diet, but families attempting to follow a Mediterranean diet may find it particularly beneficial. The following are some pointers for Mediterranean diet meal planning:

· Make a food plan in advance. This will assist you in avoiding bad decisions when you're pressed for time.
· Ensure that there are plenty of fruits, veggies, and whole grains in your meals. A nutritious

Mediterranean diet starts with these items.

· Opt for lean protein sources including beans, poultry, and fish.

· Reduce the amount of processed meals, sweetened beverages, and harmful fats you consume.

· Make as many meals as you can at home. This allows you to have more control over the components of your meal.

7.3 Troubleshooting Typical Issues

The following advice might help you overcome typical obstacles that you could run across while attempting to encourage your children to eat healthfully:

- Fruits and vegetables are disliked by my children. Attempt presenting fruits and veggies to children in various ways. You may provide them with fruit salad, smoothies, or vegetable soup, for instance. Another option is to try concealing fruits and veggies in other meals, such as yogurt or oatmeal.
- My children have a finicky diet. Remain persistent! Continue to provide your children with nutritious meals even if they first refuse them. They could eventually change their minds. My kids are always requesting junk food snacks. Give your children wholesome snacks like whole-grain crackers, yogurt, fruits, and veggies. · My kids always want to eat out. You may also try preparing your nutritious snacks, such as fruit leather or homemade granola bars. Although

eating out might be difficult, there are methods to make it more healthful.

10489187R10085